Secrets
of a Successful Loss Prevention Career.

Herman O. Laskey Jr, LPQ, CFI

iUniverse, Inc.
Bloomington

Secrets of a Successful Loss Prevention Career

iUniverse books may be ordered through booksellers or by contacting:

iUniverse
1663 Liberty Drive
Bloomington, IN 47403
www.iuniverse.com
1-800-Authors (1-800-288-4677)

ISBN: 978-1-4620-3220-4 (sc)
ISBN: 978-1-4620-3222-8 (e)
ISBN: 978-1-4620-3221-1 (dj)

Library of Congress Control Number: 2011910886

Printed in the United States of America

iUniverse rev. date: 8/2/2011

Contents

Biography

Herman O. Laskey Jr, LPQ, CFI
Owner and CEO of Laskco Inc
Regional Investigator-13 years.
Major sporting goods retailer.

Herman Laskey is a man with great expertise in the field of Loss Prevention. His 17 year career has led him to successfully aide in prosecuting over 3,000 internal and external theft cases in six different states. He has worked for three major retailers and has since started his own Loss Prevention consulting company. (Laskco Inc) He received his A.A. in Criminal Justice from Rose State College in 1996 and holds various certifications such as LPQ (Loss Prevention Qualified) and CFI, (Certified Forensic Interviewer) Wicklander-Zulawski Advanced Interviewing and John Reid Technique of Interviewing and Interrogation. He is also a licensed private investigator in the state of Oklahoma. Herman is a regular published contributor to "Loss Prevention" magazine and writes various articles on Loss Prevention topics such as "Phone Interviewing" and "Secrets to a Successful

Loss Prevention Career". Herman served in the United States Marine Corps from 1990-1994 during Operation Desert Storm. He also served in the Oklahoma National Guard from 1994 to 2000. This military career earned Herman numerous medals and commendations.

Herman has an enormous amount of Loss Prevention experience and is dedicated to educating retailers about external and internal theft. This knowledge is spread through his articles and through his company Laskco Inc where he has developed "The Stinor Method" of Loss Prevention. He is affectionately known throughout his major sporting goods company as "The Hermanator". Where ever Herman is working that day, you can be sure some theft issue will be brought to the light. (Internal or external)

Introduction

P lease allow me to introduce myself. My name is Herman Otis Laskey Jr and I have worked in the Loss Prevention field for the past 17 years. I have held Loss Prevention associates jobs as well as Loss Prevention jobs at the regional level. I also have owned a small Loss Prevention consulting company for many years.

I am a 38 year old black male who was born on May 17, 1972. My mother was Judith Ann Laskey and my father was Herman Otis Laskey. I was born in Oklahoma City Oklahoma and have two older sisters. My mother was murdered by my father when I was only two years old which left me and my sisters without parents. Luckily my aunt and uncle (Cleo and Theretia Bradley) adopted all of us and raised us to the best of her ability. Growing up with an alcoholic, abusive uncle always led me to seek out justice and to take up for the weaker guy.

My aunt had two sons that were very fun to have around. We still refer to each other as "brother" till this day. There were five kids in the house and we always had plenty. My aunt and uncle worked very hard and made sure all of our needs were met. My aunt eventually retired from General Motors and my uncle retired from Tinker Air Force base on the civilian side of employment.

My sisters and I grew up very disadvantaged but we somehow never let that stand in the way. My oldest sister is now a teacher and my other sister is a probation officer. Isn't it odd that we all chose fields that help society in one way or another? To help curb my need to help people, I also joined the United States Marine Corps in 1990.

I am now married and have two kids that I love very much. I am writing this book to help you better understand my career and why I cherish it so much. Thank you for purchasing this book and I sincerely hope that it helps you in furthering your career in Loss Prevention.

How I got Into Loss Prevention

My journey into the Loss Prevention field is probably like most Loss Prevention professionals. I was going to Rose State College and needed a part-time job to help with the bills. I worked in the toy department at Target store in Midwest City, Oklahoma. I had no idea what Loss Prevention was and I had never heard of it. I began to find empty CD packages tucked away behind the merchandise on the shelves and wondered what was going on. I quickly realized that there were actually people out there that stole merchandise from Target. This blew my mind and I began to challenge myself to find empty packages every day. One day I got frustrated and asked my supervisor what they were doing about these people that steal from the store. My supervisor called for a guy named Chris and introduced him to me. Chris was the Loss Prevention manager for Target and I had no idea.

Chris told me to call him at a certain extension number if I found any empty packages or saw any suspicious activity. I took him up on the offer and called him all the time. Chris began to catch more shoplifters with my help. One day Chris told me that I would be good at Loss Prevention. I told him that I was a criminal justice major at Rose State College. He told me that I should interview for a Loss Prevention associate job opening. I told him to forward my name and information so I could interview. About one month later I interviewed and got the job. I will always remember thinking to myself, "Cool, I get paid $6.25 per hour to walk around a store and do nothing." Boy was I wrong! I soon learned that Loss Prevention was very dangerous work and that it was my responsibility to wrestle these unknown people back into the store.

My very first apprehension was a seven year old boy that stole some AA batteries. I felt so bad all week because his mom was very mad at him. I needed my first stop and nothing was going to stand in the way. My second stop happened to be my fellow Loss Prevention associates uncle. His wife worked at the service desk and like some families, she had a drug addicted uncle. He had concealed about three cordless phones inside of his jacket and waived at her on the way out. This was my first chase. Of course, I was young and cocky, so I was not going to let and old man outrun me. He ran straight into the parking lot as I asked him to stop for me. The chase was on. I grabbed his jacked and slung phones and phone accessories all over the parking lot. I scrapped my knuckles something fierce and still have the scars to prove it.

My second stop was a huge 400 pound male that had severe psychological issues. The person had concealed a tube of caulk, a bandana and some dexitrim diet pills inside of his overalls. He was amazingly calm in the office. I began to ask him why he stole and he explained to me that God told him that it was alright. He went on to explain that God talks to him all the time and he can take whatever he wants with God's permission. I did not disagree or try to argue with him since the Loss Prevention office was only about a six by six room in the back of the store. I calmly told him that I understood. He began to tell me all of the medication that he was on which was too many for me to list in this book. He stayed very peaceful and then I began to smell a horrible stench. I knew it was not me because I had showered before work that day. I talked with him and pretended to smell nothing. The police arrived and took him into custody and I was very relieved.

I will skip a few of my apprehensions and tell you all about the good ones. One Christmas Eve I was working and noticed a clean cut attractive female selecting numerous CDs and placing them in her cart. I followed her around until she concealed all of the CDs. The female came back to the office and offered to pay for the merchandise but that was not in our policy so I called 911. While we were waiting for the police to arrive, she entertained me with a series of attempted bribes. None of them came close to my paycheck amount so I refused them all. She was the owner of a local insurance agency and felt very confident she could convince me to let her go. She tried everything from offering me a job to writing me a $1500 check. The officer arrived and was in a very bad mood. Probably because he had to work Christmas Eve. He immediately told her to stand up and placed hand cuffs on her. She was arrested for theft and taken to jail. We ran the cameras back to see what car she was driving. At closing, her car was still in the parking lot so I decided to go and take a look. Her car was filled with Christmas gifts for her kids. They would have to wait until mom got out of jail to get their gifts. I later found out that she spent all of the holidays in jail because the judges were out of town and no court was held.

Myths about Internal Theft

INTERNAL THEFT 70%?

For years Loss Prevention professionals have said that the majority of theft is internal. Is it really so? Let's think for a minute. One of your colleges is known for catching many shoplifters. Don't they always have their fare share of internals? Also, don't your colleges that have a significant amount of internals have their fare share of externals? What is this deal about 70% of theft being internal?

Some have said that one internal equals five externals. Can't the same be said for external theft? Cashiers and other employees can easily steal more than shoplifters because they are in the store on a regular basis. I have also known some shoplifters to be in the stores on a regular basis. Just because we do not see them every time does not mean they are not in the store. We simply get lucky and one day our schedules collide with the shoplifters. I personally had one shoplifter that was apprehended for $2,005. Later employees told me that he was a regular customer for years. I can tell you that his activities incurred a higher dollar amount from that particular store than any cashier in my district.

All of the culprits that print up false receipts, fraudulent checks and false upc (universal product code) codes all depend on shoplifters and are classified as external theft. These guys make six figures a years and it is all due to the shoplifters coming into the stores, not cashiers or employees. The organized theft rings depend on shoplifters to supply their inventory. These guys also make six figures a year. How many internal cases have you encountered where the terminated employee was making $100,000 doing fraudulent refunds or passing merchandise?

Yes, there are stores that have a large dollar amount of internal theft. Cashiers can pass merchandise all days long and eventually someone will notice. It may be Loss prevention, managers or a fellow employee. Shoplifters can go to any store on any given day. Let's keep in mind that some of the same shoplifters you chased out of your store were apprehended at the store across town. Shoplifters have many targets. When one store has been depleted of the product of there choice, they simply go to another store. Cashiers are fired and terminated, never to cause a loss at any store in that chain again. They may apply at another retailer but sooner or later a background check will catch up with them. We do not have the choice to refuse shoplifters entry to our stores, unless we know they are shoplifters. How often do we know this?

Some stores do have more internal theft but as a chain, this 70% theory does not hold true. Remember this when you see the figures for 2004 on internal and external theft. Believing that your chain has a 70% internal theft rate can be misleading for you, your staff and the future success of your company. One last thought to ponder is that in 2003, over 35,500 employees were apprehended which was a 7.74% decrease from 2002. The total value of the recoveries also dropped by 3.84%. The number of shoplifters in 2003 rose by 3.01% to almost 337,000. The total value of recoveries rose by 4.68%. If this trend continues it will definitely be 70% but this time the 70% will represent external theft.

31 Loss Prevention Topics

Here is a list of Loss Prevention topics for you to use at your convenience. These are factors that the everyday retail professionals do not know. These topics can be discussed at any meeting to help raise awareness. They are sure to spark conversations in every retail environment. I have chosen 31 so you will have one to discuss each day.

This list encompasses all Loss Prevention topics listed below:

1. Internal Theft.
2. External Theft.
3. Retail Statistics.
4. Discount Abuse.
5. Risk Factors of Internal Theft.
6. Risk Factor of External Theft.
7. Penalties of External Theft.
8. Penalties of Internal Theft.
9. Safety Factors of Apprehending Shoplifters.
10. Psychology of Shoplifting.

31 LOSS PREVENTION TOPICS
BY LASKCO INC.

1. Customer service is always the best form of deterring shoplifters.

2. For every $100 stolen, it takes $2,500 worth of sales to make up for the loss.

$5,000 loss=$125,000 in sales.

30,000 loss=$750,000 in sales.

3. Theft affects every employee in the end. (Raises, bonuses, etc...)

4. Knowing about theft and not reporting it makes you just as guilty.

5. There is no profile or description for shoplifters. All races, creeds and colors commit acts of shoplifting.

6. Employee theft can be anonymously reported by using a LP hotline.

7. Loss Prevention is every employee's job.

8. Shoplifters get caught once every forty-nine times.

9. Most shoplifters get the same high as drug users when shoplifting.

10. Shoplifters and employees that steal have the money to pay for the items 90% of the time.

11. Shoplifting has doubled since 1996.

12. Shoplifting is a 35 billion dollar a year industry. That is 35 million dollars per day.

13. Approximately 27 million people shoplift per year. That is 1 in 11 people in the United States.

14. Only about 3% of all shoplifters are true professionals that steal for a living.

15. 89% of kids say they know other kids who shoplift.

16. Shoplifting incidents increase about 11% per year.

17. Losses due to theft are passed on to you the consumer.

18. Most employees feel they cannot do anything about shoplifters in their store. Not true. Customer service is the best method.

19. Most shoplifters are not violent; they just want to get away from the scene as soon as possible.

20. Abusing your employee discount can cause the company losses in profit.

21. About 9% of all returns are fraudulent.

22. Chasing shoplifters through the parking lot is dangerous and should be against company policy.

23. There is nothing that your employer sells that is worth risking your career or life over.

24. Shoplifting occurs more often but employee theft results in more dollars lost.

25. Some employees risk their yearly salaries by stealing small amounts. ($49.99 Nike shoes vs. $30,000 salary) It is not worth the risk.

26. Some employees are not aware that most companies have sophisticated computer auditing systems that routinely look for signs of employee theft. (Cash refunds, passing merchandise, excessive discounts, etc....)

27. There is no good time for shoplifting. It can occur early in the morning or late at night. It can occur when the store is crowded or when there are only two customers in the store.

28. Most customers that are banned from the store just go to the nearest location and steal.

29. Many retailers have prosecuted the same shoplifters numerous times at different store locations.

30. Helping friends steal merchandise can also land you in jail for being an accomplice.

31. Most people who commit acts of theft do not truly realize the penalties for doing so.

Risk VS Gain Theory

This risk versus gain theory is used to help combat internal theft. I have found that discussing this with employees greatly reduces their potential to steal from employers. It is a fact that most employees do not consider the punishments and risks when they think about stealing from their employer. They risk stealing a $100 pair of shoes and loose their $20,000 to $30,000 salary. Most retail managers make around $40,000 to $60,000 per year. They would have to steal double that amount to make it worth the risk.

For instance, I interviewed a part time employee who stole a $179 fishing reel. He told me that he made around $20,000 per year plus medical benefits. We discussed whether or not he thought about getting caught. The thought never crossed his mind even though he admitted he knew he was doing wrong. We continued to discuss the numbers and I took a sheet of paper and wrote down $179. I also took a sheet of paper and wrote down $20,000. The employee was asked which amount he would prefer to have. He overwhelming chose the $20,000 sheet of paper. I asked him, "If we would have had this talk at the beginning of his employment, do you think you would have stolen that reel?" He told me, "I would have left that reel in the store."

We also discussed the fact that the $179 reel could have come from his $20,000 salary and he would still have $15,900 to pay his bills. He seemed very disappointed when he heard this. It is all common sense but the wrong messages are sent out to employees regarding employee theft. It seems to me that the message is "Don't steal or you will get caught" when it should be "Don't steal because it is not worth the risk." Employees risk so much when they become dishonest. Here is a list of risk factors that can be discussed with employees:

1. Your employment.

2. Your reputation.

3. Your salary.

4. Your Future.

Five Important Things to Know about Your Employees

<hr>

We all think that we really know a person after working with them for a number of years. The fact is that we never really know a person deep down inside. As an employer it is very important that we dig down deep and really get to know our employees. Knowing your employees can help give you clues about their real personality. I once had a case where a 14 year employee was stealing gas from his employer. This happened during a huge increase in oil prices so you can imagine what the employee's motive was. (To save money of gasoline) Once I revealed that the employee was stealing gas, I was sure that he would be terminated for theft if not prosecuted for embezzlement. This employee was given a two week suspension and I was asked not to report my findings to local law enforcement. The company also failed to have me check further into prior thefts of gasoline. It all seemed to me that they did not want to know. My question was "Who was going to pay for all of the stolen gasoline?"

1. Are my employees married or single?

2. Do my employees have kids?

3. What are my employee's hobbies?

4. Do my employees feel comfortable bringing issues to me?

5. Do my employees think I care about them?

The number one important thing to know about your employee is if he is married or not. If that person has a family, it makes you more aware of his or her needs at Christmas time or any other time of need. It also can give you clues if something is missing or just quite not right. For instance, if they are having marital problems they will not be as effective or motivated as usual. An unconcerned employer may think they are just being lazy that day. At any rate, they will appreciate your concern for their personal issues. Ignoring these signs may make them bitter and disgruntled. A disgruntled employee's first thought is a reckless disregard for their employer's assets.

The second important concern is making sure that you know how many kids they have. This will also help you resolve or assist with any theft or family issues that may arise. Imagine that you are an infant clothing store and you are missing numerous infant shoes. You would obviously suspect employees with infants first and then eliminate them from your investigation. I have encountered many issues where managers have released single employees with no kids early to go party when employees with kids stood by and watched. This can also make your employee disgruntled. It makes them feel that you do not care about them. If they feel that you are not concerned about them, how concerned do you think they will be about your assets? (Not very concerned at all)

The third important thing to know about your employee is what their hobbies are. That is why this is usually listed on all job applications. This particular employee may request off every Tuesday for a soccer tournament. Another employee may request off just for the hell of it on the same Tuesday. It makes good sense to let the employee with the soccer tournament off since soccer is obviously near and dear to his heart. A concerned employer that is aware of this person's hobbies will also be kept closer to his employee's heart. If any dishonest situation presents itself in the workplace, the employee will consider this small action taken by his employer and hopefully make the right decision. (Not to steal)

The fourth and second most important thing to know about your employee is if they feel comfortable bringing issues to you. In all of my 17 years of Loss Prevention, I have found that if there is any dishonest activity going on, the employees know about it. The key is getting them to come forward with those issues. You have to make sure they feel comfortable bringing any issue to you. You must then make sure you handle that issue or they will never bring other issues to you again. As I discussed earlier, I felt appalled that the employee stealing gasoline only got a two week suspension. I am a 17 year seasoned veteran of Loss prevention and the thought still crossed my mind. "Why bring issues to them if they are not going to thoroughly handle them"

The fifth and most important thing to know about your

employees is making sure that they know you care about all of the topics you just read about. Most employees get through the day by telling themselves, "This is just a job." I would rather my employees tell themselves, "This is just a job but my boss really cares about me, my family and my hobbies."

Using Deterrent Pages to Deter External Theft

Deterrent Pages

eterrent pages are utilized to combat external theft in your stores. The store should be divided into three zones. (A, B, C or 1, 2, 3) Since all stores are not the same please refrain from using the departments to establish your zones. Each employee should memorize all three zones and know what type of merchandise is kept in that zone.

Generally, the left side of the building to the first main aisle should be Zone 1 or A. The middle section of the building which is all of Apparel should be Zone 2 or B. Finally, the right side of the building from the main aisle ending at the reel bar should be Zone 3 or C. The zones should have an imaginary line that runs all the way to the back of the building.

All deterrent pages should be repeated every 2 to 3 minutes until the issue has been resolved. Remember to change the zones and give the correct zone if the suspected shoplifter changes departments. This will be another tool to make all associates aware of possible shoplifters in the store. When the pages are heard, all associates should cease all projects and immediately roam their zones to look for suspicious behavior. No customers should be ignored and as always, customer service is the best deterrent.

Here are some examples of practical uses of the Deterrent Page.

Scenario 1

1. An associate notices a repeat shoplifter enter the store and heads to the pocket knives. The associate will page, "Security Scan Zone 3."

2. An associate working top stock on the Marine aisle will immediately cease his work and roam the entire Zone 3 giving customer service and looking for suspicious behavior.

3. Another associate zoning on the Archery aisle will cease his work and roam the same aisle giving customer service and looking for suspicious behavior.

4. The suspected shoplifter and other customers should be approached by two associates which will either help the honest customers find what they need or deter the suspected shoplifter.

Scenario 2

1. A Footwear associate notices a pair of old shoes on the floor and a new pair of Nike shoes are missing.

2. The associate pages, "Security Scan Zone 1" and begins to roam Zone 1 giving customer service and looking for the new pair of Nike Shox.

3. A Team Sports associate is stocking basketball goals on the basketball aisle and ceases all work. He roams his zone and notices a customer wearing a new pair of Nike Shox.

4. The Footwear associate also notices a customer and approaches him to give customer service. The customer has been approached by two associates and returns to Footwear looking for his old shoes.

Deterrent pages are not guaranteed to work in all cases; however, having a set routine to deter theft will give associates and management more confidence in dealing with what is naturally an uncomfortable situation.

A great way to reduce your liability on external theft

W e have all read numerous articles about the dangers of exposing your company to lawsuits by pursuing shoplifters. I want to dispel some of those myths by giving you more confidence in dealing with shoplifters. After all, the problem of external theft exists in every retail environment and ignoring it will not make it go away.

Some retailers have it written in their policy to not notify law enforcement until the perpetrator is in custody. This causes several problems. The first is that you and your fellow employees have to risk getting hurt while subduing or escorting the suspect back to the office. Secondly, you might get caught in the old quiche of "bringing a knife to a gunfight". Police officers are ready and prepared for all hostile situations. I cannot say this for most Loss Prevention personnel. With the exception of a few retailers, most only carry handcuffs.

Every Loss Prevention professional has that one that got away.

Notifying the police early can help prevent this. Of course we should be careful and not get itchy dialing fingers as soon as we think a suspect is about to do something dishonest. We have to see a crime committed before our very eyes. Listed below are some key details and instructions that can help you and your company catch that one that got away. Using this procedure has helped me secure some of my largest external apprehensions.

1. Observe the suspect approach the item.

2. Observe the subject select the item.

3. Observe the subject conceal the item.

4. Call 911 and inform them of the events taking place.

5. Maintain constant visibility of the suspect.

6. Approach the subject when they exit the store with police witnessing everything.

7. Escort police to the subject if they arrive early and enter the store.

If the subject is apprehended inside of the store, police may not arrest them. This depends on the local shoplifting statutes and the police officer. I have had officers arrest the subjects numerous times without the subject leaving the store. The main point to remember here is that it does not matter. The shoplifters did not get away with your merchandise and that should be the main goal.

You must also be aware that they might have a getaway car waiting on them. I normally have an associate assist me by checking the parking lot for such a car. Here are some of the signs to look for in the parking lot.

1. Cars double-parked or parked in the handicap parking spot with no visible handicap tag.

2. Car backed into parking spaces. This enables them to have a quick getaway.

3. Cars parked right outside the front doors. I usually ask if they are waiting for a large bulk item to be carried out. (Grills, ping-pong tables, patio furniture, etc...)

4. Cars parked in the very back of your parking lot by the main street. This also enables a quick getaway.

5. Cars that have one or several occupants and they are watching the front door of your store.

It is a good idea to record the tag, make and model of these vehicles in case they do get away. This information is very important and can be given to police dispatch to help the officer identify the car.

The most important thing to remember about this article is these 911 calls will serve as great evidence of a crime. In today's turbulent economy that is ripe with copious frivolous lawsuits, a 911 recording should and will serve as great evidence to derail any lawsuit brought forward by dishonest customers and employees. After all, these recordings are public record and can easily be obtained by attorneys representing your company.

A Pocket Guide to Conducting a Successful Phone Interview

Phone interviews can be used in any situation; however, there are numerous situations where a phone interview can be most effective. Conducting an interview over the phone can lead to a quick resolution of large and small issues. There are many pros and cons of conducting phone interviews. In this article, I will discuss them and give reasons why or why not they can be proven.

Here are several cons for conducting phone interviews.

1. I can't see the subject's facial expressions or gestures.

2. The subject cannot see me to establish rapport.

3. There is no substitute for a face to face interview.

4. I am just not good at phone interviews.

Try to visualize the subject during the interview. This can be achieved by getting a photo of the subject or just viewing

CCTV. Gather facts from the staff that is present. You can ask questions such as the following: How old is the subject? How many kids do they have? What type of demeanor does the subject normally display? Asking and knowing this answers can help you visualize the subject during the interview.

Rapport can be established in any situation. Some experts say that communication is 75% non-verbal. Use that 25% of verbal communication to ask questions that general are conversation starters. Here are a few good examples. How is the weather in your town or city? Did you see that game last night? How is your day going so far? These questions can psychologically put your subject at ease before you start asking the tough questions.

Face to face interviews are very effective; however, some subjects can be intimidated by a very seasoned interviewer's appearance. This can cause them to shut down and not give any information. Over the phone, you can make choose what type of interviewer you want to portray by sounding stern or sounding very friendly. It also lets the subject's imagination run wild thinking of a face to pair you with. This gives them less time to think of false stories and denials.

Like anything else, phone interviews need to be practiced. The more you do, the better you will become. Approach it with a positive attitude. This always makes me think of my 10 year old son when I hear someone say, "I am just not good at that." It will be a change for some but just remember that it is an additional skill in your arsenal. Imagine only taking one gun into battle. You at least show be armed with the knowledge knowing how to use all other weapons on the battlefield.

Phone interviews can also save your company $1,000 dollars at a time. Imagine you have an employee on video that just pocketed $50.00. You can book a trip and handle it days later or you can set up a phone interview. In my vast experience, a subject will either confess or not confess. How many times have you planned a trip to handle a huge case only to come up empty handed? If you come up empty handed on a phone interview, your company is not out of any money.

Now I will discuss the Phone Interview Checklist. This list should be checked off before conducting any phone interviews.

1. Control the amount of people in the room during the interview.

2. Gather personal facts about the subject being interviewed. CCTV can help in doing so.

3. Brief all witnesses in the room before starting the interview.

4. Make sure the subject is setting close to the speaker phone and never have him pick up the phone.

Controlling the amount of people in the room can be helpful in limiting interruptions. You do not want the subject to feel intimidated or distracted in any way. This can also limit your liability if the case goes to court.

Make sure you know who your subject is. This will help you to establish rapport and also let the person know that you did your homework. Imagine that you are interviewing a very large individual and he is suspected of stealing a size small article of clothing.

Briefing your witnesses is very important to reduce liability. Some witnesses can get overzealous and may have a personal connection to the subject. Also, the subject may turn to them for help or ask questions. Explain to all witnesses that they should remain quiet and not respond to comments or answer any questions. This is very important even after you are done with the interview. Some witnesses may want to help and make promises that we are not aware of.

Before you began to talk to the subject, make sure he is setting closest to the speakerphone. This gives the conversation more intimacy and makes the subject aware that he is the main focus of your dialogue. It also allows him to tune out other things happening in the room or outside of the room.

Conducting phone interviews in today's economy can greatly reduce your company's expenses. I did a short six month test and realized that I had the lowest amount of expenses in my department. This gave me more time to do other things like walk the sales floor and build rapport with managers and associates. In closing, if you have a boss like mine, you will receive accolades for limiting your expenses and not hopping on a plane at the drop of a hat.

This guide was written to help Loss Prevention professionals enhance their careers. In my 15 year Loss Prevention career, I have learned numerous things. One important thing is making my days at work efficient. We can spend a whole day just planning a trip to travel and handle a case. Phone interviews can be very efficient if properly planned. It is not simply a matter of picking up the phone and gathering the accused with managers in the office. Just like any other interview you must plan ahead and prepare for unforeseen event and denials.

Let's just think for a minute about the cost of traveling to a location to handle a case. You first have to factor in the time spent investigating the case. Then there is the issue of which mode of transportation will carry you to your destination. Now let's figure out the cost of a hotel room if the issue requires more than one day. We all have to eat at least twice a day which will increase your expenses. Now let's imagine a clean cut case where the subject is on CCTV. (Closed Circuit Television) If the subject does not confess and he knows he is on video committing the act, he probably will not confess at all. So should we take a chance and increase our monthly expenses or should this case be handled with minimum investment?

Investigation hours-2 to 4 hours minimum.

Rental car-$20 to $40 per day.

Airfare-$150 to $400 round trip.

Fuel or mileage paid by your company-$10 to $30 round trip depending on the location.

Hotel-$60 to $100 per night.

Meals-$30 per day minimum.

Becoming proficient at phone interviewing can be viewed as

you making money for your company. We can invest anywhere between $300 to $600 traveling to handle a case. Phone interviewing can reduce your company's investment by 100%. This directly makes your company more profitable by reducing your Loss Prevention departments cost of doing our business. After all, profitability is every business's main goal. A trained Loss Prevention professional can easily handle a clean cut $1,000 case without leaving the office. Here are a few examples of the benefit of being proficient at phone interviewing.

Dealing with the report aspect of phone interviewing

1. Be prepared to write a report and fax it to the store or office.

2. Assign a person to make the report.

In some municipalities, the officer may need a statement from the person who actually did the interview. Be prepared and have a statement ready. Be sure to include key details so that others further down the law enforcement chain will know that this was in fact a phone interview. It will help push the case along. If someone confessed to stealing over a speakerphone, it is pretty much a closed case. This makes it hard for them to say they were intimidated by you.

Other municipalities my not want the interviewers information and want someone who is on the scene and heard the interview. This is fine as well. Just make sure that the law enforcement appointed reporting person includes all details. It may be better to write the statement for them and have them sign it if they agree with what is written. This ensures that you know all of the details in case it goes to court.

Whatever the case, you should always know what is in the statement. In the end, you are ultimately responsible for the entire case.

Case Studies

O ne day I received a call from one of my stores that was approximately 2 hours away from my home store. A manager recognized an employee that he worked with at a store across town. He saw that the employee was conducting a return with no receipt. It was a $300 GPS. The manager called his old store and talked to the employee's supervisor. Apparently the employee had just gone on his break and would have to return to work. I instructed the manager to watch video of the reel bar just before the employee's break time. Luckily we found that the employee had concealed the GPS inside of his jacket and left the store. I began to assign duties to the witness for my interview and we waited for him to return. In the mean time, I gathered all of the suspect's information to aid me in the interview. The employee arrived and we started the interview. He confessed to stealing the $300.00 GPS and two other items which brought the total to over $1,000.

I could have planned a trip to this city and risked him not showing up for work the next day. However, I saved my company approximately $300.00 and prosecuted a $1,000 case. This also save my company payroll for my travel time and let me focus on developing other cases. This case was handled free of charge.

There was another case where an associate noticed a fellow employee wearing old shoes in the morning when they arrived. During break time he noticed that the employee was wearing brand new Nike Shox. He reported this to management immediately and sent me the video times so I could remotely access the video. It was very clear to me that the employee did not pay for the new shoes. Once again, I followed my process for conducting a successful phone interview and obtained a confession. The Nike Shox was $119.00.

My hotel room alone would have cost $119.00. This particular store was five hours away and would have required me to fly. I estimate that a trip to the store would have cost my company $700.00. Ponder this for a moment. $700.00 for a pair of $119.00 shoes. Once you do the math it makes more sense to become proficient at conducting phone interviews.

Cost associated with face to face interviewing.

With the majority of companies' slashes Loss Prevention budgets it is very important to keep your expenses down. Phone interviewing can easily help you do this. We must first discuss all of the possible expenses that come with doing interviews.

1. Travel time.

2. Mode of transportation or mileage rate.

3. Airfare costs.

4. Lodging costs.

5. Meals.

Travel time can vary depending on your area of responsibility. If the store is close to you a face to face interview is recommended. When all of the criteria are met to conduct a phone interview, you must consider doing so. Do not forget that you also have to get back home which doubles your travel time. We normally only work 8 hours per day so a four hour trip will burn up half of your day. Every hour spent traveling is one hour that could be spent in the office being productive. Always double your travel time right of the bat to help you better estimate your time.

Driving to your destination is always cheaper for your company; however, a long drive is not always the best thing for your body. The average mileage rate paid to you is around 45 cents per mile. A 250 mile trip could cost your company over $200 round trip. Using a rental car could cost around $35 per day plus an additional $20 to $50 in gas. If you have an interview that meets the criteria for a phone interview, consider doing so to wipe out these expenses.

Plane tickets can easily make your expenses sky rocket. $200 is about the lowest price for a round trip these days. As Loss Prevention professionals we sometimes have to pay that high dollar last minute plane ticket. Let's not forget about the rising taxes and security fees involved. Unless you have a ride from the airport you will need to rent a car and purchase fuel for the car. Renting the car adds to your travel time and most travel time is time that you are not being productive. If the criteria are met for a phone interview you can wipe out these costs and be on to your next case.

Lodging costs are very necessary. The average decent hotel room will cost at least $70 to $90 per night. If you are on a long trip you will need a room to recuperate. We have all had cases that led to more interviews which may require you to stay additional days. Traveling to handle a case is very unpredictable.

Keep in mind that lodging costs can easily double depending on the scope of your case. Choosing to conduct a phone interview can wipe out this expense and after all you have the room already set up so just keep on rolling!

Imagine that you have just gotten a confession on a huge case and you are feeling very confident. Don't you feel entitled to a nice meal? Most meal budgets are $35 to $40 per day. Let's face it; who is going to turn down a good free meal? Not me. In my travels I have found all of then good food places. My boss jokes about how I can find the best food places in any city. Needless to say we are going to eat good on the road and it won't be cheap. If you choose to conduct a phone interview you may already have you lunch in the office with you. Depending how the interview goes you can have lunch right after you get your confession and it will not be at the expense of your company.

These are all of these expenses that we should think about before making travel plans for any case. I highly recommend that you keep track of your phone interview cases and list all expenses that you saved your company. Here is a simple format that you can use. Include this sheet in your case files for future use. This will show how much your company is spending to handle cases and how much they can save by training all employees to conduct phone interviews.

CASE NUMBER-2010-46783.
AMOUNT-$387.62.
INTERVIEW TIME-1 HOUR.
MONEY SAVED.
-AIRFARE-$250.

-RENTAL CAR-$100.
-GAS-$50.00
-LODGING-$75.00
-MEALS-$40.00

TOTAL SAVED-**$515.00**

The Stinor Method

USING THE STINOR METHOD IN COURT

As Loss Prevention professionals we sometimes have to appear in court to testify. Although our cases are not like the O.J. trial, however, they can result in judgments equal to the O.J. civil trial. Our company policies tell us to review the report and dress nice. We rely on our experience and the fact that we know what we saw. How would you like to have a set protocol for trial? There has been a system set up for Loss Prevention professionals and regular employees to follow. This system was developed and marketed in 2010.

Beware of attorneys that will attack your experience and creditability. I want to discuss several factors that aid defense attorneys in winning their cases against retailers.

1. **Your experience**- The less time you have in Loss Prevention, the more they will attack you.

2. **Your company policy**-Make sure you never violate company

policy on the witness stand. Once they have confirmed that company policy was violated, it can make everything else you say questionable.

3. **Your recollection**-Be specific about what happen and when it happened. If you make a slight error on dates and times, it can be used to discredit the rest of you testimony.

We hope that you never have to testify in court for one of your employees having a bad apprehension. In fact, the Stinor Method was developed to keep retailers out of court. It is always better to be prepared. In my years of testifying, I have never lost one case. This was possible because I always stuck with my method. I have heard horror stories about defense attorneys turning the tables on Loss Prevention professionals. One thing that always stood out to me is that they never have a consistent method or game plan when they testify. My goal is to have all retailers rely on the Stinor Method if they have to testify in court. The Stinor Method is legal and clear cut. It has no discrimination, profiling or singling out of any certain race or gender. The Stinor Method will soon become the secret weapon of retailers that face scrutiny in court. Our goal is to have defense attorneys shaking in their boots when they hear that the retailer used the Stinor Method. I will also be available to testify for you if necessary.

Stealing by shoplifters and employees cost retail businesses over $14 billion dollars every year and is listed by the FBI as the fastest growing crime in the USA. Shoplifting and employee theft reduce the average retailer's profit margins by 40% and is responsible for a reduction in total sales of at least 5% per year. What this means financially is if you are a retailer doing one million dollars per year in gross sale, shoplifting and employee theft are costing you $50,000 in lost sales per year!

The STINOR Method Loss Prevention Program is a proven system for reducing shoplifting and employee theft by up to 95%. The STINOR Method has been used for over 15 years by thousands of retailers and restaurants and it is considered to be the most effective loss prevention system ever developed.

With The STINOR Method Loss Prevention Program, you will reduce shoplifting and employee theft at your retail business by up to 95% in 90 days or less, guaranteed, or we will give you a 100% money-back refund.

Every retailer and their employees should know what shrink is and where it comes from. Shrink is defined as a reduction of inventory due to shoplifting, employee theft, paperwork errors and vendor fraud. Most retailers have a difficult time finding out where their shrink originates. Due to the latest technological advances we have exception reporting systems to help aid in achieving this. Shrink basically means that you and your company are going to loose profit. Using the Stinor Method gives a clear game plan on reducing your shrink.

Sources of Shrink

43.7%-Internal Theft
32.6%-External Theft
12.9%-Administrative Errors
5.4%-Vendor Fraud
9%-Unknown

The percentage of loss of products between manufacture and point of sale is called shrinkage. The average shrink percentage in the retail industry is around 1% to 2% of sales. While that may sound low, shrinkage cost U.S. retailers over $31 billion in 2001 according to the National Retail Security Survey on retail theft. Here are the some of the major sources of inventory shrinkage in retail.

1. Employee Theft

According to the National Retail Security Survey, the most common source of shrinkage for a retail business is internal theft. Some of the types of employee theft include discount fraud, refund fraud and even credit card abuse.

2. Shoplifting

Coming is second place is <u>shoplifting</u>. Customer theft occurs through concealment, altering or switching price tags, or transfer from one container to another. Shoplifting remains a smaller inventory loss source than employee theft but stealing by shoppers still costs retailers about $10 billion annually.

3. Administrative Error

Administrative and paperwork errors make up approximately 10% to15% of shrinkage. Simple pricing mistakes can cost retailers quite a bit.

4. Vendor Fraud

The smallest percentage of shrink is vendor fraud or theft. Retailers report that vendor fraud occurs most when outside vendors stock inventory or delivery it directly to the store.

My Five Secrets to Succeeding
In Loss Prevention

In my 15 years of Loss Prevention I have learned many things but none are more important than having a passion for Loss Prevention. Passion separates extraordinary people from normal people. This is true for any field or work or expertise. Many professionals could easily make their own characteristics of a successful Loss Prevention career and you would be hard pressed not to find passion in their top five.

1. **Passion**
2. **Certifications**
3. **Think like a thief**
4. **Be patient**
5. **Do it all**

1. **Passion**-Passion is defined as any powerful or compelling emotion or feeling, as love or hate. You should attempt to love Loss Prevention as much as you love your family and friends. Loss Prevention should be in your daily vocabulary.

Amongst your family and friends, your profession should not be a mystery.

2. **Certifications**-There are numerous certifications for the Loss Prevention field. (LPQ, LPC, CFI) Certainly any Loss Prevention professional can do his or her job without certifications. This does not make it a waste of time. Certifications are a clear sign of going above and beyond. It helps your superiors realize that you are serious about your job and want to continue learning. These certifications can be researched by going to the Loss Prevention Foundation website. I will leave you with these words that I once wrote in an article. "A certification may be just a piece of paper but it is a piece of paper that everyone in Loss Prevention wishes they had."

3. **Think like a thief**-Most great Loss Prevention professionals would make great thieves. We tend to think out of the box and anticipate a thieves' next move. Once a shoplifter steals a piece of merchandise, you must think how that person is going to benefits from that theft. Is he going to the flee market? Is he going to sell it to his neighbor? Is he going to return that item at another store in your area? A hunter must know the behavior of the animal he is hunting or his trips to the forest will not be fruitful.

4. **Be Patient**-Patience is a virtue. Promotions will come in time. We cannot jump from job to job hoping to slide up the corporate ladder. I once became impatient at my first Loss Prevention job and left the company to make only one dollar more an hour with another retailer. That company that I went to filed chapter 11 and went out of business 1 year later. I so regret

leaving my first company. That was over 10 years ago and my sincere regrets have yet to leave my brain. I later learned that my major issue with the first company was resolved less than one year later. Had I stayed and outlasted the issue, I would be making much more money today. Just keep in mind that you are able to outlast temporary setbacks.

5. **Do it all**-Do not be a one trick pony. Be concerned about all theft. (Internal and external) Once in my career, I was known for only catching shoplifters. I expanded my horizons and later became known for conducting successful phone interviews and have since published an article on this topic. Later, I became known for having a knack for building rapport with store employees. This was achieved by asking my peers for help. People are not afraid to share their talents. It is very flattering in most cases. It is okay for you to love one aspect of your job but it is a career killer to continue to focus and build on that one aspect that you love so dearly.

There are many other secrets to having a successful Loss Prevention career and as I discussed earlier, any great Loss Prevention professional could easily make their own list. What is absolutely true is that not having goals and secrets to enhance your career can hinder your success in Loss Prevention.

Types of Fraudulent Refunders-
S. U. L. F.

E xpert refund fraud companies estimate that approximately 9% of all retail refunds are fraudulent. In this article, I want to discuss the types of fraudulent refunders and familiarize you with their methods. I also want to introduce the acronym "S. U. L. F."

SULF is used to help heighten awareness of refund fraud.

There are four types of refunders that seriously affect a company's refund policy.

1. Selectors-This type of refunder usually enter the store empty handed and selects merchandise.

2. Users-This type of refunder tends to borrow merchandise for a period of time and then return the item with their original receipt.

3. Losers-This type of refunder usually shoplifts merchandise and return it with no receipt.

4. Fraudulent receipt-This type of refunder is highly skilled in printing counterfeit receipts.

Selectors

Selectors are the second most common type of refunder. They are very skilled at entering the store undetected. They may wear hats or sunglasses to help alter their appearance. Selectors will enter the store empty handed and select merchandise from the shelf. This person might even walk by the front door or call for a manager to give the appearance of entering the store with the item. Selectors are easily deterred by an alert manager reviewing the front door camera. In most of my cases, the refunder will immediately leave the store without the merchandise once he realizes that the front door cameras are being reviewed.

Users

Users are somewhat common and these people, in most cases are not shoplifters. They have figured out a way to save money and feel they have done nothing wrong. Users hide under the customer service factor. All retailers want to meet their customer's needs and will exchange or refund an item to make the customer happy. Retailers are normally not concerned about users because the manufacturer allows a credit for damaged or used items.

Losers

Losers are the most common type of refunder. They will

shoplift items and later return them for a store credit. Losers are notorious for losing their receipt. They concoct stories of about receiving the item as a gift from their grandmother who lives far far away. Losers are very harmful to a company's inventory and shrink number. When they steal the item it causes a loss and when they return the item, it inflates the inventory.

Fraudulent receipt refunders are rare, however, they can do allot of damaged. They never work alone. They normally have a group of shoplifters to steal the items and collect sku numbers for them. The shoplifters will return the items with a very realistic receipt. Very few retailers will question any refund that is accompanied by a receipt. Retailers can detect this type of refund fraud by noticing the same types of items being returned for cash.

Characteristics of a Fraudulent Return

In this day and age we are hesitant to profile anything. Whether or not you agree with profiling, most cannot argue with it end results. Profiling has been given a negative image by society. Had the 911 hijackers been profiled, the worst terrorist event in history may not have happened. Instead of profiling we just pick out certain characteristics and focus on those in hopes of good results.

In retail there is a huge problem with fraudulent refunders. Refund experts say that only about 9% of all refunds are fraudulent. This approximated 9% can be reduced by making note of and recognizing the similar characteristics. I am going to discuss them in this article to help you do so. What retailer does not want even a 1% increase in sales?

Some retailers ignore this 9% and just call it the cost of doing business. Others use the excuse that most customers are honest and they don't want to punish honest customers by tightening up on their refund policy. Having worked in the Loss Prevention field for almost 17 years, I had the luxury of seeing these interactions with honest customers. Most of them understand and expect nothing for free while others get upset and leave the store. These customer claim that they will never shop in your business again only to return the next time they have a pressing need for your product. I have also heard of cases where they attempt to poison the well by telling their friends and family about their bad experiences. These cases are rebutted but the friend or family member being puzzled since they have never experienced such an issue.

1. The first characteristic is that most fraudulent refunds are not accompanied by a receipt. Shoplifters routinely return items to get a different size or style.

2. The second most common characteristic is that most shoplifters will return like items that are of various sizes and styles. It may be five shirts that range from small to large. The shoplifters story will go something like, "I decided not to buy some many so I would like my money back. Some will even state your return policy and challenge you on it.

3. The third characteristic is that shoplifters always have conflicting stories. At first they purchased it last week, then last month and finally, they did not purchase it at all. "It was a gift from my dear old grandmother." This flows with the old saying, "It's always easier to remember the truth but it is very difficult to remember a lie."

4. The fourth characteristic is that most fraudulent returners return used or damaged items. The product may be faded from

being washed numerous times. They also return items that have creased or damaged packages. They may have had to fold it or squeeze it into a purse to get it out of the store. It is also difficult to get a package concealed in their waistband which can easily explain damaged packaging.

5. The last most common characteristic is that some stores routinely return the same merchandise not having the sales to reflect such a sale. You may gaze over and see that the display is empty. You may then check sales only to find that you have not sold any at all. This can create a positive inventory in your store. You have zero on the display and 5 on the books or in your inventory system. When you return one that was stolen, this gives you a false count of 6. You actually only have one that you just returned. This may get a little tricky but take a few moments and think about it. After all, shoplifters spend more than a few moments thinking about how to steal from you.

Having just two of these common characteristics can give a retailer enough reason to deny a refund and deter the shoplifter from stealing it in the first place. If they know your company will refund it, they will continue to steal it. Make no mistake, dishonest customers are more aware and educated on your return policy than most of your employees.

Deterring Theft in the Fitting Rooms and Bathrooms

etailers all face a common threat of having their merchandise stolen in the fitting rooms and bathrooms. Some even have policy strictly prohibiting apprehensions if the suspected shoplifter enters the fitting room or bathroom. While the exact percentage of fitting room thefts cannot be measured, it remains a consistent threat. I have encountered many scenarios that could have resulted in lawsuits. It is a good idea for you to establish a set policy on attending the fitting rooms.

There was one case where a lady had concealed numerous CDs in her purse and went to the bathroom. Although I could hear the plastic being torn off of the packages, I could not see her conceal the product. She exited the bathroom and I found no evidence. It could have been flush down the toilet or just concealed it a great hiding spot. I stopped the customer outside of the store and escorted her to the security office. I asked her to surrender all of the stolen merchandise and she opened her purse. Much to my surprise, her purse was empty! My heart began to beat very rapidly and all I could think about was losing my job due to a bad apprehension. I immediately informed the lady that I was going to notify the police and they would ultimately search her for their protection. The lady ran out of the office never to be seen again.

This case could have easily resulted in a lawsuit and me losing my job. Luckily I was an experienced but young Loss Prevention agent and knew the right action to take. It is actually some retailer's policy to apologize and let the customer exit the store.

I want to share this training with you to help assist you in your fight against shrink. This should serve as a guide to help you establish some sort of policy in your store.

FITTING ROOM ATTENDANT TRAINING

1. Position your employees where customers can see them.

> **A.** Behind the desk.

> **B.** At a folding table.

2. Greet every customer entering the fitting room and make eye contact.

> **A.** Hello Sir or Mame, how many items will you be trying on today?

3. Visually inspect and count all items.

> **A.** This deters draping. **(Draping-The act of using Apparel**

items to conceal footwear, electronics, pocket knives and other high theft merchandise prior to entering the fitting rooms.)

4. Thank all customers when they exit and make eye contact.

  A. Immediately offer to take the clothing back to the sales floor for them.

  B. Enter the fitting room and inspect it for loose tags or hangers. (This should be done after use of all fitting rooms)

Please make sure that all shopping carts are left outside so it will not block access to the fitting room. Allow customers to take their strollers and car seats into the rooms if there is a child inside of it. All strollers and car seats should be <u>visually</u> inspected.

If a customer exits the fitting rooms without his or her merchandise, check the rooms immediately for tags and hangers. Notify management immediately and make a false security page. (Security Scan Apparel or Security to the Fitting Rooms)

My Time in Cuffs

I t was a sunny, brisk week day afternoon when I had stopped by my office to file some papers away. I was eager to get home so that I might enjoy fishing at Lake Hefner later that evening. I did not look for any action, nor did I want any that evening. Fate was working over time that day and my fate was sealed tight.

A very alert employee somehow got word that I was present that day and paged me overhead to call her extension. I reluctantly called her back and asked if there was a situation. The employee informed me that there was a very drunk Hispanic male trying on boots in the Footwear department. I told her to talk to him and make sure that he received the best customer service that she could provide.

I later walked out of my office and checked the situation out myself. There he was a very inebriated Hispanic male that was trying on a pair of $119.99 Justin work boots. I surmised that he blood alcohol level prevented him from noticing the bright, white security tag on the left boot strap. He placed his old rugged, decomposing boots in the new box and concealed it in the very back of the shelf. My natural instinct took over and I forgot about my pending fishing trip that I had planned for later that day.

I called 911 and told them that I had a theft in progress. They were also alerted to the man's condition which was less than sobering. The suspect walked through camping with the new boots glaring on his feet. I thought to myself, "Maybe I can just get the boots from him and let the Edmond police deal with the public drunkenness issue." Boy was I wrong.

The suspect approached the front exit door and I attempted to identify myself as he kept walking. I told the man, "Just give me my boots and you can go". The subject picked up the pace and ran out of the store. This upset me since I was going to cut him some slack and afford him one less criminal charge for that day. I immediately called 911 and informed them that I had a runner. I watched as he made a hard right turn and headed for the railroad tracks just west of the store. He saw that I was watching him and ran into a wooded area next to the tracks. My guess is that the woods were too dense for him so he immerged from the woods and headed back to the railroad tracks. This time he was wearing only white socks. Close your eyes and image a shoplifter running down some railroad tracks in white tube socks.

I saw that the police were headed up the railroad tracks in the direction of the fleeing suspect so I knew that he would be apprehended. They eventually caught up to him in a field so I walked back to the store. The railroad tracks were difficult to walk on so I decided to take shorter route behind a bank. After all, the bank was only two businesses down from the store. As I walked behind the bank, an armed Sheriffs Deputy sprang out of the back door of the bank and ordered me to put me hands up and get on the ground. I of course had to comply since his gun was drawn and ready for action. As he cuffed me, he blurted out many violent phrases that gave him assurance I would not move. One such phrase was "If you move, I will blow your fucking head off!"

While setting in handcuffs in the rear of the bank, I noticed employees peering out of the windows and doors at me. This humiliated me to a huge degree. I began to explain to the Deputy that I was walking back from a shoplifting incident and he could call The Edmond Police department to confirm this. I explained the situation in detail and urged him to call Edmond police. The deputy told me that he heard chatter over his radio about a theft and he thought it was me. I told him that the suspect was a Hispanic male, not a black male. The police arrived and a familiar officer walked up to us and asked the Deputy what I was doing in handcuffs. The office told the deputy who I was and that the shoplifter had been apprehended already.

Needless to say the deputy was very embarrassed and released me from the handcuffs. In all of my 38 years of life, that was my first in handcuffs. I guess anyone can have an experience like this one. (Even a seasoned veteran in the Loss Prevention field) Strangely, I routinely see this officer at the mall near my home. I am sure he recognizes me as I recognize all of the people I have apprehended.

Thank you page.

I would like to give a very special thanks to Academy Sports and Outdoors. I have been employed as a Regional Loss Prevention Investigator for the past 14 years. Academy is where I honed my Loss Prevention skills. When I started with Academy, we had no security tags or cameras. Needless to say it was a haven for shoplifters and dishonest employees. Our Loss Prevention department changed on a yearly basis which prepared me for an eventful career. I mastered every new policy and task that was required of me. Some of these tasks helped make me a better Loss Prevention professional and made me work outside of my comfort zone. I began to try new things ahead of time. We never had a set policy on how to accomplish a certain task so we just did it the best way we knew how.

My current VP of Loss Prevention is Joe Matthews. Joe was always very good at letting us do what we were good at. He understood that he had numerous Loss Prevention professionals and we each had our own special skills. This attitude helped us and gave us the flexibility to continue to do what we were good at. We were not forced to conform to a set protocol of doing our jobs the same way. This is what makes some jobs mundane. Joe, if you are reading this, "Thanks for the flexibility, it made me a better Loss Prevention professional."

I would also like to thank every employee at Academy that helped me in a case whether it was external or internal. Employees have always been a very important part of my success in Loss Prevention. Maintaining good communication with employees is never really talked about in the Loss Prevention field, however, it should be focused on more if you want a successful Loss Prevention career. To every Academy employee I have ever worked with, "Thank you very much. Your cooperation and interest in Loss Prevention issues is much appreciated."